THE TWELVE-FOOT NEON WOMAN

LORETTA COLLINS KLOBAH

THE TWELVE-FOOT NEON WOMAN

P E E P A L   T R E E

First published in Great Britain in 2011
Peepal Tree Press Ltd
17 King's Avenue
Leeds LS6 1QS
UK

ISBN 13: 9781845231842

Supported by
**ARTS COUNCIL
ENGLAND**

ACKNOWLEDGEMENTS

Several of these poems have been previously published in journals and an anthology:

The Caribbean Writer: "Cereus of the Night Passages", "Two Women Chatting by the Sea (1856)", "The First Day of Hurricane Season", "El Velorio, The Wake (1893)", "The Twelve Foot Neon Woman on Top of Marla's Exotik Pleasure Palace Speaks of Papayas, Hurricanes, and Wakes" and "Reading *Krik? Krak!* in Puerto Rico"; *Poui: The Cave Hill Literary Annual:* "After Hurricane Lenny, Carriacou", "By the Waters of St. Lucia", "Canute Caliste", "Snort This", "Matron", "Peckham, London, Cold Water Flat", "Night Wash" and "Caribbean Art"; *Cimarron Review*: "Ladies Room, Chicago Bus Terminal"; *New Caribbean Poetry* (Carcanet): "Going Up, Going Down", "Novena a La Reina María Lionza", "Two Women Chatting by the Sea (1856)", "The First Day of Hurricane Season" and "El Velorio, The Wake (1893)".

SPECIAL ACKNOWLEDGEMENTS

My gratitude to mentors and poets whose *talleres,* discussions, or friendship have impacted my book: Philip Levine, Mervyn Morris, Kei Miller, Victor Hernández Cruz, Willie Perdomo, Lorna Goodison, Elidio la Torre Lagares, Kamau Brathwaite, Larry Levis, William Matthews, Marvin Bell, Gerald Stern, Jorie Graham, Yolanda Rivera, Dannabang Kuwabong, María Soledad Rodríguez, Christian Campbell and Ishion Hutchinson.

Give thanks to academics Victor Chang, Eddie Baugh, Nadi Edwards, Carolyn Cooper, Gordon Rohlehr, Mary Lou Emery, Margaret Bass, Reinhard Sander, Lowell Fiet, María Cristina Rodríguez, Alma Simounet and Leah Rosenberg.

Jah bless: Sandra Echevarría, The Fire This Time-dubdem, Casper Loma-Da-Wa, Modesto Cepeda (¡BOMBA!), Graffitero Ske, aka Eliezer Pagán, and the FX TNB Crew, Mas' man Michael La Rose (son of John), Mrs. Pat Morgan, the late Trevor Rhone, the late Lawrence Noel of Trinbago Carnival Club and London Calypso King Lord Cloak.

Thank you to Kwame Dawes, Jeremy Poynting, Hannah Bannister and Adam Lowe of Peepal Tree Press.

Love to my children, Jeremy and Wenmimareba.

CONTENTS

Yo puertorriqueño soy,
profesión esperanza.

– Tite Curet Alonso,
sung by El Sonero Mayor,
Ismael Rivera

CEREUS OF THE NIGHT PASSAGES
Viejo San Juan

          El Cristo de Buen Viaje,
washed ashore from a shipwreck in the 18th century,
dragged from the Atlantic coast of El Morro to the chapel
by devout residents of El Callejón de la Capilla –
bloody kneed Christ, who bore his green tree of a cross
over the ragged sea bottom. Christ, with red anthuriums
and a lone peacock feather piled at his feet, draws no
attention from the Señora. Thin, dressed in headtie
and belted housecoat, she bends over the small fire
of her prayers and then stretches on her toes to reach
the high ledge where she releases a bundle, crumpled
in her fist, at the feet of San Martín de los pobres.
It is not her rosewood rosary or a plea scrawled
in compressed script across a vanilla sheet,
but one wilted white bud.
          In El Callejón, one balcony
strung like a cuatro prevents seven trembling palomas
from perching, from singing their cantos to the borrachos
gathering below, under the awnings of El Corazón.
Oh, from that window to hear the sea breeze whirl through
the callejón and strum the nylon strings. To hear the growl
of raw quarrels between the pigeons and drunkards.
The window is shuttered. Behind it, the antique lamp, the bed,
the key on the bed stand, the great half moon of the aguacate.
The wick of the oil lamp flickers, the epiglottis of a drunkard
gulping its blue fuel. A girl's linen gown lies on the floor,
a crumpled white bud.
          Under the rains of wet season,
in dark, glistening, blue-bricked callejón, we knot
together under black umbrellas. When the jazz musicians
tossed us out of their club, we pushed out into the rain,
lingering, tethered to the spot. Young poets climbed up
to the precipice, a narrow ledge of the snaking alley walls.

Three in the morning, we still stand in the downpour,
the pobres of La Perla, the rum shop cabrones,
and poets, in the gleaming, blue-bricked, cold streets.
I wrap my dress around me like waterlogged wings.
I hear the nimble young poets declaim their poems.
I watch their papers drawn crumpled, and folded,
and melted from pants pockets. Through half-shuttered
lids, I see them opening into the night, wet buds.

LA MADONNA URBANA

The dusk sky wore a corona of doves
                coasting over Los Dos Picos,
                      the two pink, pointed breasts
            of la Iglesia de Dios Pentecostal
of Barrio Obrero in Santurce.
On this Isla encantada de Puerto Rico,
on La Calle Lima, is where it began,
        at an hour when Prospero's Tire Center
                had locked up (donde las gomas usadas
                      no tienen garantía), and El Bohio Bar
              boomed its bachata bashment.

Maybe it started as a breeze
        off the water at the marina Los Laguneros,
            spiriting past the gutted Pinto jacked-up on concrete blocks,
                the burned out school bus. Maybe it was only vapour
                    gliding past una gallina that ran in the road
                  with its pollitos in La Buena Vista,
    eddying around an albino girl playing
        basketball in la cancha de un residencial,
two snakes of smoke drifting through a game of dominos in the park.

Doña Doris, with a bag of cilantro, garlic, carrots, corn, peppers,
      and yautía from El Colmado Plaza Borinquén
        under her arm, was tired. She had come from the bus.
She was walking home. She was the first to see the lips move.

There, at the back wall of the Colmado,
                   where graffitero SKE and the FX TNB crew
had spray-painted the twelve-foot woman onto the wall, bust portrait
framed by a graffiti spell of petroglifos geométricos
           that called her spirit to the wall,
        Ske had painted her hair con el sabor del café del campo,
           one highlighted strand at the forehead made of golden rum;

13

her dark brows and shadowed eyes sweet-talking and cockfighting;
　　　　　her lips pressed closed, unsmiling;
　　　　　　　　　her scooped blouse off-shoulder,
　　　showing rhinestoned pink bra strap, abundant breasts.

Our Lady of Barrio Obrero, la señora profana, la madonna boricua,
　　　　　la cabrona, la Gata,
　　this María, with street credentials painted just in front
　　　　　　　　of la Iglesia de Dios Pentecostal,
　　　where, after storms, in shadowed night,
　　　　　flooded streets turn into pools of sparkling light,
　　　　　　　and the hard working campesinos de las clases empobrecidas
　　　　　　　　　　listen in their beds
　　　　　　　to maracas of gun shots a las tres de la madrugada.
　　　　　　　　　　　They lie in bed thinking that those shots
　　　　　　are not disparos al aire, but are meant to put bullets into someone
　　　　　　　　　　　　　so that he will die before morning.

When the lips of the mural first moved a little, and the tongue darted out,
　　　　　　the faint sound was like the stir of a lady's Spanish fan,
　　　　　　　a spider spinning in the inner nave of a guitar,
　　　　　the butterfly kites of El Morro fluttering against the ocean air.
　　　　　Then　quietly　came　　*Ay*, *Lei Lo Lai　Lei Lo Lai*

¡Ay, Señor! ¡Ave María! Doña Doris exclaimed and ran home to make love
　　　　　to her husband three times in arabesque positions,
　　　　　　　so she did not hear Our Lady
　　　　　　　　chanting the litany written on the wall of El Colmado:
　　　　　　　Sandy, Cuajo, Goldo, Manuelito, Felipe, Glock, Chuola,
　　　　　　　La bicha, Boricua grita paro nacional, el 15 de octubre,
　　　　　　　las mujeres somos putas y puercas, William-n-Nadira,
　　　　　　　　Facundo Recordz, 100 X 35, Shakira pendeja,
　　　　　　　　　　¡Coño!

To Jorge in fishing galoshes and sweat-soused shirt,
　　　　　　　　　　carting his pole over his shoulder,

the lips whispered: *Busca para la vía de la esperanza.*
To Coraly with a boy child on her hip,
      la Madonna Urbana sang Bob Marley's "No Woman No Cry".
To José in the sun, mending his hat with needle and thread on the curb:
                                        Chivas Whiskey
To Alejandra skipping from the church in choir robe:
      Tienes que ser una mujer con pantalones.
To Melba, community activist at 23 years old,
      dueña of an ecotourism microempresa and defender
          of the communities of El Caño Martin Peña:
        Bendición   *Give thanks*

To Juanito, who limps barefooted on sun-melted asphalt
      and drags his bad leg at the crossroads, our Legba,
whose open sore festering from knee to ankle has not healed in a year,
      whose wound is unbandaged in the dusty street,
         whose affliction is deep and wide
with ruffled edges of fat and meat around the opening,
      whose leg we motorists have watched gradually turn colour
            from trigueño to darkest black,
whose torn McDonald's cup we put money into day after day
      because we know he is going to die soon,
          sin velorio, sin baquiné,
and the money that we all endlessly work for will not stop that,
      or the hour of our own death;
          to Juanito, who, nonetheless is still singing
            at our car windows as we wait for a stoplight
              to turn the colour of the yankee dollar;
to Juanito who wears yellow rubber starfish earrings in both ears
      and says, *Mamita, se ve bién, que linda eres*
          and *Mira, tengo hambre;*

Juanito, the only one to notice
      that sometimes Our Lady's hair also moves,
         tossing like in a Clairol commercial,
         making the air of Barrio Obrero taste of tamarindo;

to Juanito: *descansa.*

breathe.   never get weary yet.   alma, espíritu y cuerpo.

Graffiti Madonna cries out to us: *Pa'lante, Pa'lante, como un elefante.*

As the barrio sleeps, Our Lady of Providence and Juanito sing to us
with the voice of Ismael Rivera: *Las caras lindas, las caras lindas,*
las caras lindas de mi gente negra. Oyeme, pero que bonitas son, lindas son,
chulas son, bonitas son, lindas que son, lindas como tú verás, así son.

THE FIRST DAY OF HURRICANE SEASON

My daughter still sleeps in late morning light
slanting through the jalousies and cresting
waves on a coverlet batiked with flying fish and manta rays.
The salt of her damp neck tastes like pumpkin seed husks
as I kiss her and ease from the bed.
I dress in a loose shift, a faded indigo blue button-down
that I used to clasp with a belt, or a man's
cupped hands as he stood behind me in the kitchen,
warming me with his morning "pointing finger".
The salt shakers danced as I braced against the table.
A woman in middle years, I crave solitude and earth tones.
The high arched white walls and the ochre floor tiles
of my sun-polished front room please me.
Canvas, clay, driftwood, sediment, shell, and dirt.
Outside the window, the flamboyán flares its scarlet
skirt like the flamenco dolls sold in seaside boutiques.
Bristling with curled silver Spanish moss, and assuming
the knurled bonsai pose that I once admired in cypress trees
held fast to outcroppings on the Californian coast,
the tree shelters ground doves. Heat clogging the veins
of its dry, cracking heart, my flamboyant tree survives,
solitary on a street named Los Flamboyanes
for the once vibrant red satin-lined boulevard of torch trees
and fallen blossoms. Lizards run and leap along the roots,
small black ones, brown, blue-streaked, and the ruffle-bearded
iguanas that undulate in motion. A summer morning.
I brew fresh ginger tea with coarse brown cane sugar,
cut a papaya, and watch the sun bead its juices.
No one ever taught me to expect that a phase of life
spent without a lover could be as happy, simple, and rich
as this. Now I am remembering just the way his pelvis
swung hard and loaded with freight into my labia
flame-petals. The memory feels good, like fireworks
in the kegel muscle and quick-spreading heat.
The tossed seas of my own body in humidity
and golden air kindle both satisfaction and peace.

EL VELORIO, THE WAKE (1893)
— a child's wake in rural Puerto Rico

In Puerto Rico's most famous painting,
El Velorio, a carved pig crucified
on the ceiling beams surveys the crude
beauty of a child's wake, the grey
doll laid out like a bride in its floral wreath
and lace, and los jíbaros indulging
in a baquiné with excesses of spirit and flesh.
The plenitude of green plantains
and dried corn hanging from the rafters
of the wood-beam and thatch room
show this to be a home of simple provisions.
A low-slung leather Taino chair pushes back
empty from the table, as if the owner
might have risen temporarily to take some
refreshments or air, walking casually through
the open door, past the grazing cattle
and the coffee plantations, and over the hill,
and into the sea. An old African,
head banded, feet bare, and legs crippled,
has his own perspective, looking
down at the baby gathering its halo
of flies. Children brawl on the floor
over calabashes of spilled food
while the babe's mother pours out wine
for the priests. The cuatro and güiro play on.
Playing cards strewn on the floor
might symbolize the superstitious
faith of the jíbaro, the tarot pack,
and bets taken over which neighbour might
provide the next occasion for a country wake.

*   *   *

Did Yashira, playing in the back of a pickup
with two cousins in a rural sector of Corozal,
see the bala perdida in flight, the great cosmic bullet
the news media described as "stray", as if
it had become lost from its mother, disoriented
and determined to be useful, to penetrate any
flesh in its path? The paper does not mention gun
or culprit, just the anonymous bullet, which
entered Yashira's stomach, exited her back,
and continued on its blind flight.
Six years old, she had appraised
our world wisely enough to tell la abuela,
Me voy a morir as she ran to the house
and fell at the threshold. At the home wake,
Osiris Meléndez López, the disconsolate
young mother, brushed her child's hair,
sang and talked to Yashira, rearranging her clothes
for the journey, kissing her goodnight.
This girl, too, was adorned in head wreath and veils.
Juan Ramón, the father, lifted his small bride from the casket,
carrying her to the balcony. In the street, 600 neighbours,
who had come to pay respects, vomited, ran away,
and cried so that the mourning was heard fifty meters away.
He raged, *Miren a mi bebé, ella es mi hijita querida,*
while seven municipal workers laid asphalt
on the driveway where Yashira rode her bicycle.
This visual detail, added to the parent's home
in tribute, will remind them daily of the absence.
Like the Taíno chair pushed back from the table,
the bicycle will never again seat its owner.
Juan Ramón walked on his knees through wet asphalt
to the funeral service at a nearby church.
We have created a new world where the indiscriminate gun
is always at our backs. From the first murdered Taíno to now,
the cosmic bullet has been in the air. The carved moon
trots across the sky. Let us rock our babies

to sleep, kissing their hair, rearranging
their night clothes, playing our odds against
carnage, against the stray shot seeking our thresholds.

SNORT THIS

There is something to admire about a precision cut,
you say, as you line up the white powder on glass.

The precision of the evisceration suggested a keen
medical knowledge: which internal organs

to remove, which to leave. The incision carving
a half-circle on Yohaira's abdomen was precise.

When police found her body bound in blood-soaked
sheets in the backseat of a car travelling erratically

in Bayamón, the driver called her his sleeping wife.
Driving manuals should make it explicitly clear:

When driving with a dead drug mule in the backseat,
obey all rules of the road, have the tail-lights

repaired, remember haste makes waste.
Before Yohaira Giménez decided that

cocaine-packed condoms and chocolate pudding
make a rich meal, she was somebody's daughter.

She drew pictures of pájaros and palm trees.
Haven't you noticed, on those pleasure trips

to the sunshine isles, that the Caribbean
woman's body is a beautiful thing?

Yesmarie Pérez Fernández lived in a wooden house,
subject to attack by mice and wild weather.

Comadre to a fifteen year-old, did she expect
to be undone by a boy she had helped raise?

A swarm of heroin addicts determined to steal
a small pension cheque can be innovative.

Other women might hope to explore higher
states of sensual bliss at sixty-nine years old.

I hope to be at peace, comfortable with my body,
reserving it for the garden, new shoots of plantains,

pepper plants, scallions, and coco yams to tend.
Let me curse roosters and goats away from my legs

as I take long walks to the market for okra and tamarind.
At night, I shall brew teas from the guanábana leaf.

Yesmarie, 69, sexually violated with a plastic tube
by these addicts, nearly bit her tongue in half.

Maybe she was somebody's mother once.
She was somebody's daughter. Her hair

was oiled and braided and swept up from her face.
She was photographed while chasing a hermit crab.

Someone watched her push the arroz y gandules
around on her plate. When she fell sick, Tía

blended aloe vera, honey, garlic, limes, onions
y agua for her to drink. You might say that at least

Yohaira had the benefit of a quick precision cut.
Switch on the TV, crank up the MTV video.

You can almost feel the saltwater spray
in your face from the speedboat chase,

and the helicopter adds the perfect effect
to the bass beat. The drug business is glamorous,

if we believe the videos and switch off the news —
the cocaine bales jettisoned overboard in haste,

the archipelagoes of floating cargo lacing the Caribbean sea.
I think about these two women — not about

bullet-riddled boys littering the streets of el barrio.
Need a little something to take the edge off?

You know where you keep it, go ahead. Get wired. Relax.

AFTER HURRICANE LENNY, CARRIACOU

Surf mists through sliding glass door

Black hills of the invisible night sea
alive – colossal sound

Stunned curtains whisk up
salt atomized in air

Bare bulb on the wall

This room – the sea's new causeway

Wavelets enter, scour floor tile – wash back

No steps to the beach, no sand – all washed away

Sea at the threshold
surging freely into the room
No barrier –
Building anchored in sand
might give way, might put out to sea
while you sleep

Mesmerized, wet, leave the door open
Smell the clean tang, the reek

Water tumbler, Iron Jack, no ice
on the nightstand
Burrow under coverlet
Switch off the light
Night was never as total as this –
gulping sea all around

Trust Miss Lucille to take the helm

Norfolk Library and Information Service

Please keep your receipt

Borrowed Items 04/01/2017 18:22
XXXXXXXXXX2357

Item Title	Due Date
The twelve-foot neon man. [paperback]	25/01/2017

indicates items borrowed today
Thankyou for using self service
THANK YOU FOR USING
NORFOLK LIBRARIES
You can renew items online
Spydus Mobile phone app
by phone at 0344 800 8020
Ask staff about email alerts
before books become overdue

BY THE WATERS OF ST. LUCIA

> *... and the dispossessed*
> *said the rosary of islands for three hundred years*
> — Derek Walcott, "The Star-Apple Kingdom"

The library is locked, but behind the grillwork windows
slant antique volumes carried from Rome to this island enclave
where iguanas scrawl their own missals in moonlight and sand.

The Benedictine Sisters of St. Lucia let my daughter ride
their skirts, work habits of canvas, old sails of tall ship *Brig Unicorn*
cut to size; she tugs their skirts from kitchen to stone altar,
absorbing the blaze of hearth, of hand-baked guava tarts,
and sun-hallowed light of the stained-glass St. Scholastica.

From the greenweb of bush forest, the clearing of the monastery
offers a woman space to rest near the shade of prickly pear,
pumpkin vines and stone fish pond. Offers a small girl room
to tilt her face to rain, trouble Sammy the guard dog, and spy
sailboats and puddle-hoppers descending on Castries.

We do what others do, take a tour to Choiseul, Vieux Fort,
Soufrière, the volcano's bilging sulphur, boiling dark water.
The driver dismisses Walcott's allusion to the conical Piton
mountains as Helen's serene breasts. *A poet has his own way*
of seeing, the Pitons are miles apart.

We cross the island, through villages
of wooden houses open to the weather, where, says the guide,
politicians appear before elections and then vanish. *Work? What work?*
In Soufrière, we see the government-built lockers
for the fishermen, salt-rusted zinc and screen-wire lean-tos.

In Anse la Raye, where street vendors sell blackened corn and whelks,
and country & western music plays, we eat a seasoned fish,
wrapped in foil and stewed in its juices, and roasted breadfruit.
For me, Walcott's lines, poorly remembered, filter rain forests
and fishing villages, Rastafari and schoolgirls along the narrow road.

My daughter loves the nuns. She watches them halve oranges
and squeeze the juice into a pitcher. I ask Sister Emmanuela
nothing about the slaughtered Irish nun, the damaged church,
or the men who styled themselves as Rasta and burned Babylon.
Who am I to balance anyone's heart against a feather?

Women from two islands far from Zion, we talk
while a three-year old girl runs everywhere,
making a Sister look at her reflection in a gold doorknob,
leaving a naked, armless Barbie doll in the sanctuary.

When we go home to Puerto Rico, everyday a young man
will recite his litany at our window, *Missy, some change*
for food, medicine, or *drogas*. He will show his one bad foot,
where bloody lesions boil into small volcanic mountains.
I used to want to ask where his mother was.
Now some days I give change, some I don't.
After days of downpour in the wet season,
he will greet me on the corner, a foil windshield
protector held over his head like a small galvanized roof.
Missy, how do I look? Like so many other
street people in advanced stages of SIDA.

He will die one day in the street. He will sleep
on the steps of El Ladrillo Bar and wake
to pains that rock him. All morning he will rock himself
on the sidewalk as my neighbours and I do nothing.
Someone will finally call the police. They will arrive
on bicycles and then scribble notes on clipboards
while he rocks and tucks into a foetal ball.

Before he is cleared from the street,
an *El Nuevo Día* photographer might snap
his feet soles curled together like a sleeping infant's.

My daughter tells a Sister that she wants
to be a mermaid with a long tail. On the plane, she will
see mermaids in cloud-nets cast by Martinique,
and the tourists in the seat behind us will ask of saintly islands,
from St. Vincent to St. Thomas, *Is that Puerto Rico?*
It looks more affluent than St. Lucia from the air.
On descent, my daughter and I will glimpse our street
of red flamboyán trees, where a bearded man
kicks a rosary of fallen flame blossoms.
Scarlet, purple, and blood-black sores bloom on his legs.
Sunset, he walks from window to window,
hailing each María to bestow upon him a small grace.
For a short time, we will be above it all.

CANUTE CALISTE

In Carriacou, the granddaughter
of Mr. Canute Caliste – master Quadrille
fiddler and intuitive painter –
tells me that mermaids do not come in
as close to shore as they used to,
preferring the security of their caves
near Union Island or Petit Martinique.
They no longer put themselves on view.
His wife lifts dough loaves into the yard oven.
He builds fishing boats or walks
by himself on the sand at Fontabelle,
where surf-hammered coral and conches
mosaic the beach after a storm.
Mermaids once lifted their heads to peep
at him – bobbing like a handful
of yellow sea roses in surf.
He paints the sea and sporting whales,
mermaids in their gardens and sharks,
the building and blessing of the boats,
sugar cane and the green mountains,
big drum nation dances and donkey races,
weddings and extramarital affairs,
"Jackluar" devils and the Shakespeare mas',
his own yard and tomb feasts,
and again and again, in bright colours,
the revolution and US invasion of Grenada.
In this one, he has labelled
buildings at Fort Rupert "arrested here"
or "killed here". Somewhere
in the line-up of men marching
at gunpoint, Maurice Bishop
vanishes from the scene,
perhaps rising in the dark smoke
issuing from the fort's canons

as two black helicopters swoop.
Mr. Caliste has not painted
the basketball backstop against
which Prime Minister Bishop stood.
Grass-studded soil does not divulge
how executioners disposed of his remains.
Students seem to be at panicked play,
tossing themselves to the ground
long enough to register the shock
of the shots, and perhaps
the shapes of Caliste's words already
embrace them: "Stedunt died
on the groun with guns shrt all died."
From the high fortress wall, tumble
five bodies, their surprised appendages
flailing like starfish legs, turning
like pinwheels. Small, black figures –
children of the revo – fly backwards
into the rocks below or the sea.
Sea foam gleams like new jewels,
frothy dreams uttered by the hoarse
voice of the sea. Mr. Caliste signs
the watercolour, "My Memory Alwy There".

MATRON

Eighty years old and pretty,
walnut-skinned school nurse
with rolled-cotton hair,
starched in white uniform,
ready for the children's ruses
of monthly cramps and headaches brought
on to escape their exams, Matron
believes in good governance.
She has one rule at home:
no men. And so she has lived
in sanctuary and light for forty years
since her husband cleared out.
When I saw what men could do to women,
I gave up on them entirely.
When man-worries stress me,
she boils the soursop leaf for sleep
and strains the sweet pulp fruit
with grated nutmeg and vanilla
into a milky balm to soothe me.
What is for you cannot be unfor you.
Nothing was ever so true. Only once
in those forty years, a man dared raise
his hat at her, *a gardener, and smile, just so,*
and say something facety, like men do.
She kissed teeth and wheeled about-face.
She nursed her children and her garden
on her own. She took her nurse training
in England, where her school mates asked
how one manages to cook in Jamaica.
I have no time for foolishness.
When Michael Manley died
and was ceremoniously motorcaded
through the streets and mourned
by Fidel Castro and his entourage,

30

she said the man tried to build
a country with the broom. *Rastas*
take their street-sweeping jobs
in the government reform and turn
street-sleeper. Cho'! She sleeps
early, through the drums from
the Twelve Tribes yard, the sound system
deejay bawls and the crowd's gun salutes.
She wakes at three a.m. for solitude
and tea. She drinks a monthly foul
aloe vera purge. We share a simple evening
repast of boiled pumpkin and beef bones,
ackee and salt fish, or rice and peas.
Positioned at the table to see *Young and the Restless*,
she laughs loudly at the intrigues of *too-wicked-Jill*.
At night Matron patrols the patio before bed.
She cracks the croaker lizard's back with a stick.
When her well-to-do son drops by *once*,
in all the time I rent a room from her,
to hand her a bag of green Seville oranges
through the iron gate, she cries.

GOING UP, GOING DOWN

for Ricky, Richard, Miguel, Joel, Dávid y Walter

This is a poem that can't get published – in the Caribbean –
– in Puerto Rico, in St. Croix, in Barbados, in Jamaica,
       in St. Lucia
  I just bet you three lotto tickets that it can't.

This is a poem that has to roam, has to scavenge,
      has to live in its car, has to live on air,
  has to wander the back alleys, has to curl up
      on the steps of your padlocked front door,
  has to snatch your straw purse to get a little room
      to crawl into, to breathe in –

Yes, this poem is on the run –
until the Caribbean is quite ready to greet this poem
  like we meet friends in Puerto Rico, with a besito –
  with a saludos, with an embrace.
  See what I mean?

Okay, let's leave orange grove bungalows,
  messy kitchens and plantain rows.
      Excuse me: a grander view of joy
     and liberation in Puerto Rico, a land
     where – as they say in Jamaica – batty bwoys
     are called patos –
     waddling ducks.

      In the elevator, the man's hand brushes
    against a man's jacket.
The red lights of radio towers stub out like cigarettes.
      The men drive through the privacy
of darkness, humming to Ricky Martin.
Da da da-da-da da-da, la vida loca.

The hotel is vacant.
Two scenes: one a still life in the elevator;
one in the realm of action,
            the exhilaration of speed,
            of the roaming car,
            road wind, reggaeton, and the hotel
                on the horizon.

                A night clerk reads the zodiacs.
        A poui-scented receptionist – Carmen –
        books the suite.
All the way
            to the penthouse,
            the man's hand grazes
        the jacket.
    It's raining, creating a mood of operatic awareness
            of bravery, fever, post-love aloofness.

It's like there is a soundtrack to this poem.

        The receptionist casts a seaside gaze –
        she thinks
                it's a spectacle, two men carrying
                    their love for each other
        like a shield – something to tell Papí
        about later in bed. The patos in room 216.
                She wasn't raised well.

How did these ramblings turn
    homoerotic in the tight space of the elevator, where
        I have put two men bruising accidentally against each other,
    and where I am meditating on their carnal destinations?

You can't do that, poem! Get back, Jack, back
    to where you belong, poem.
Homos don't exist in the Caribbean, poem.
    And get off the beach, poem.

33

Wrestling boys, my childhood nemeses, now holding
   briefcases under
      their arms, wrestling a cup of coffee,
        seek the afternoon terraces
      where they will loll in bathing suits,
      warming testicles in the sun.

Is it because corpses lie
      in little beds of straw in the war zones
  that I must demand
    a little tenderness between men?

That's nasty business, poem, pure nastiness.

Is it because I've seen on the evening news
men's legs that had been beaten
    with shovels by the police –
    because the men were suspected
    of being
    homosexual
        inna
          Jamaica?

This poem is not a lying poem.
This poem is an eye-witness.
That's why this poem has to be clandestine.
  This poem is in danger of being stoned –
      Nuh fling rockstone.

       Listen –
  they're in the elevator, trapped between floors.
They have not yet escaped to the other vignette,
the freewheeling car or
      the seaside tryst.

  Would you like to ask these men anything?

What do you think of the assault of
                Jane Doe
                        in Prospect Park?
        The refugee child who died
                two hours from the border?
In a boat not seaworthy, five miles from the Florida coast?
On the flooded river banks of a Haitian shanty town?
        So much to think about,
        and we have to think about patos, poem?

I rub my hands over my eyes. The men do the same.
        Do they pass the time with talk,
        stuck, as they are, in the elevator?
In the grand, airless elevator of the big Caribbean Hotel
    that presses them down, down, down, if they
    try to rise —

    What would you talk about
    if you were stuck in time? Stuck in an elevator
    especially designed for patos like you?
    For batty bwoys like you?
        About the International Monetary Fund?

    Do these men brag like Tom Arnold
            yukking it up
    at the Harley Davidson Cafe, "I've had more
            pum-pum than ex-President Clinton!
            (and that's
                a lot of pussy!)?"

No, they are better men than that. Sensitive.
    It doesn't matter. They are just men
    trying to love each other.

    Would somebody *please* get the censor in here?
        We need to censor this poem, right now!

Let the elevator rest on its proper floor
            and the door slide wide.
Let these men be themselves, to invite love in the way
                that they can.
    Even under the fluorescent glare
    of the elevator, the kiss
                is one of the sweetest they've ever known.

Or perhaps not.
    Why should they satisfy my predilections,
    utopic pleasure, safety, respect, and a Caribbean lullaby?
    A lullaby of One Love?

Nice try, poem.
    Now get off the beach. Go on, *git*.
    And don't come back, poem,
    until someone, somewhere –
    anywhere –
    in the Caribbean is brave enough
    to publish this poem.

LOTUS

Sun
varnishes a curve
of the coconut. Its mouth is
a black hole rimmed by blond fibres
bright sand has scooped out shadows
at the coconut's green bottom
dried and fallen palm fronds
tangle over the
coco
and
one
white
plastic
fork
is
on
the
sand
next
to
it

TWO WOMEN CHATTING BY THE SEA (1856)

Before Camille Pissarro left St. Thomas island
to become a father of French Impressionism,
he studied women bending to their chores,
washerwomen and water carriers, African
women of the Danish West Indies, sketched barefoot
and rooted to their tasks of lifting and cleansing
at the stone well. He had not yet added
the yellow hatchworks of light that fall
brilliantly on brightly garbed peasants
labouring in the patchwork grain fields of Pontoise.
He drafted the curvature and hoist,
the spine's taut response to the weight
of things that must be carried, the rounded
shoulders of a woman gathering bundles low
to the ground and her erect exactitude in balancing
loaded trays upon her head. One pencilled
study of a mule traces the heavy neck
swaying low and legs hobbled closely together
so that the joints bend awkwardly inward.
A workbench must have stood nearby,
but Pissarro drew only a solitary vice.
The mule and the steel clamp on a white
page beg for the viewer to interpret symbolically
the mule's burdens and constraints. Later landscapes
burn with the steady effort of leverage:
the belaboured body bowing in dashes of sunlight;
field dancers galloping in hand-clasping roundels
under a dusk sky move with the cadence of labour.
Women apple-pickers and gleaners stay in the fields
until the gold light turns indigo and then deep blue.
By the time Pissarro left St. Thomas, slave labourers
in St. Croix were rising up against their masters.
The world was starting to lose its edges,
its clear definitions of colour and order.

Even for the European bourgeoisie, painted at leisure
in the newly wrought light of the Impressionists,
nothing was certain. Whirling winds in Van Gogh's
night sky were the winds of change,
not the troubled dreams of a mystic painter
alone, but the churning of a world
adjusting its human wobble to the rhythms
of Marx, Martí, C.L.R. James and Fanon.
The son of a union unrecognized by Jewish elders,
with a Sephardic Jewish haberdasher
born in Bordeaux as a father, and a mother
about whom little is known, except that she haled
from the island of Dominica, Pissarro schooled
with the illegitimate heirs of the Danish plantations
and black children at a primary run by Moravian pastors.
As were many middle class children of the islands,
Pissarro was later sent away to boarding school in France.
We can blame him for missing the opportunity
of painting the post-slavery islands into art history,
of fleeing to peasant villages where he could escape
disdainful glances of the African women he drew
and the sellers and buyers at West Indian market squares.
In the open markets of France, people sorted cabbages
and butchered pork without thinking of the far colonies
and their freed darker-skinned counterparts toting
vegetables and calling customers in creole songs.
How tedious it must have been, though, for a young man,
returned from school to labour in his father's haberdashery.
He inventoried the staples sold to the ladies
of Charlotte Amalie and dusted shelves.
At twenty-two, he got away, sailing with painter
Fritz Melbye to Caracas, Venezuela, and then France,
where he and other vagabond artists and anarchists
noticed how the light was gradually changing.
He came to love the detailed drawings by
the Japanese artist Katsushika Kousai,

prints of artisans, the net menders,
wheelwrights, and grain grinders bowed
to their work. He began to disdain the monied classes.
In one of Pissarro's few completed paintings
depicting daily life in St. Thomas,
two women pause on a wheel-ridged path
by the sea, their backs to the whitewashed hillcrest
and the foggy surf break, where a miniature party
leisurely searches for seashells or prepares
for a Sunday feast at the water's edge.
A lady must lead the distant gathering
since someone lifts a black umbrella,
the sort carried in the Caribbean to protect fair
complexions from the salted surf bite and sun glare.
In the foreground, the African women
brace their loads; one wields a larder basket,
one an amply laden headtray draped in white
lace linen. Passing upon the path,
they have stopped out of hearing distance
from both the painter and the small party
that gazes out to sea, where no Danish prows
perturb the waves. Both wear dresses flounced
with extra yardage at the waist. The woman
in white is collared by an orange and red scarf
caught in the breeze. It could lift her up
suddenly into the air and over the hill
and away to wherever she wants to go,
if it were not for the ballast of the headtray
anchoring her to the path. Their conversation
belongs to themselves alone.

CARIBBEAN ART

Near pylons for el tren urbano, a Brazilian guava tree,
massive girder nearly petrified, raises its
concrete trunk and sparse tufts of green over
Río Piedras's botanical gardens, a space to walk
among palm groves, ponds where a red-billed
kingfisher stalks, and cool bamboo coves
laden with broken beams that creak overhead.

Here in the centre of the grounds, the designers
have replicated not the rainforests of El Yunque,
but Monet's garden, bridge arching over pools
of broad lily and lotus leaves. The water brims
with ornamental fish and red-eyed turtles,
breaking the surface with their snouts as they dog-paddle
through green water, the long moss fringing their shells
undulating like hair.

                    A gazebo and benches
invite visitors to linger, to contemplate the serenity.
A plaque explains the planners' intentions.
Monet's gardens should inspire local artists,
who are welcomed to sketch and paint the scene.

I sit here and sketch what I see rising above the ponds:
The hills of urbanization – Río Piedras' sprawl –
with their staggered masonry of concrete
and improvised wooden-slat houses painted in turquoise,
lemon yellow, and the inner-pink of conch shells.
Zinc-fenced yards and empty lots crisscross
with the broad leaf fans and waxy, bruised-pink
blossoms of banana trees. Chickens and dogs
keep company among castaway bottles, derelict mattresses.
Boys play basketball in the court behind the squat
church that parishioners have painted in basketball colours,
a bright orange with black steeple, shutters, and eaves.

READING *KRIK? KRAK!* IN PUERTO RICO

Under the vaulted ceilings of la torre,
the grand Seville clock tower, where sun
paints the archways in brilliant light
and warmth on marble floors, students
usually sleep or read, or sleep and read.
Sometimes the Conjunto de Clarinetes plays,
weak reeds gathering the heat and dust
of the tower into a somnolent splendour.
Or the strolling trovadores of the Tuna,
in crimson-lined black cloaks, black leggings,
and ballooning bloomers, strum the Islamic laúd,
bandurria, or guitarra. They crave the acoustics
of la torre as they sing about the lady love.
Perhaps, one disappointed trovador
let a sea breeze whirl up under his cape,
turning him into a vision of black butterflyhood.
Perhaps he flapped around the tower still,
as my students read "Children of the Sea"
in the last minutes before class. Four women friends
breathlessly told me it wouldn't leave them alone,
an enormous black butterfly that battered one woman's face
and would not be deterred while they read Danticat's story
under the clock tower. They batted it away and ran from it,
but it stayed on course, trying to alight in Laurita's hair.
"…and then, there it was, the black butterfly floating around us."
Jorge doodled in his art pad during class that day,
inking-in veined leaves and insets of a woman's nude back,
a pose between repose and labour, as if she were simultaneously
resting from a beating and rising up again. He replicated
her image in miniature, a morphed figurine whose spine
was composed of leaf veins, whose body assumed a chrysalis shape,
and whose arm outlined a butterfly wing: "Mariposa negra".
Students talked about tennis shoes washed ashore, dehydrated groups
of Dominicanos and Haitians routinely hunted down

by La Guardia Costera, drowned in Mona Passage,
hailed at sea, or corralled on shore
and deported from Puerto Rico. They admitted how little
they knew, though living just next door, as islands go.
From a botánica, one student bought a framed Erzulie
in her danto aspect, the African Madonna,
with three bloody scars marking her face.
"Night women" walk the barrios of San Juan, too. She wrote
a poem about a prostitute in seven skirts, blue and white, who
with her hips, rocked the tides against the walls of the old city,
lulling the deambulantes and the residents of La Perla to sleep.
After reading "1937", one woman brought a cantaloupe to class.
She said that her mother, a devotee of espiritismo, had her own
annual ceremony at the sea. In Danticat's story, she said,
Haitian women needed to remember the baptisms of blood
their mothers received in the massacre at the river.
In Puerto Rico, we remember our massacres, too,
but we try, too often, to forget. A quintet played "La Borinqueña"
while women dressed in white walked with their children and men
down a street of Ponce. We remember that one, our "1937",
when police blocked off the street, shot and clubbed Nationalistas.
Once a year, my mother writes her bitterness
into a message, and inserts it into a melon, the student said.
She prays and throws the melon into the sea. It carries
her sorrows away. In a college classroom, where wobbling
ceiling fans stirred the heat, we each wrote our messages
for the cantaloupe, according to her instructions: a memory
from Danticat's writing, a phrase, an image, an allusion,
an action, a person impossible to forget. Students
chose the crow-women of the jail and hair that sprouted
from makeshift graves, but I chose the quilt stitched
in "The Missing Peace", a royal-purple, unravelling weft.
This semester, the students read *Krik? Krak!* as closely
as they always do here, but this time they also responded
as artists and spiritualists with their own memories to craft.
Will they forget? The cantaloupe was for remembrance.

I don't know about its lasting effect as a learning tool.
I don't really want to carry this thing around all day,
and we don't have a river or beach around here,
the student told me after class. At home, I took
our messages out, cut the melon,
and thought about eating it. I didn't, though.
It was for remembrance.
The melon was so tart. It was so sweet.

LANGUAGE AND THE MAPPING OF SLAVERY

A New Account of Some Parts
of Guinea and the Slave-Trade,
by Captain William Snelgrave, 1734

Snippets of language

As to the Human Sacrifices
that part of Africa
is of a large extent
30 Minutes North Latitude
as far as the Coast of Angola
being that farthest Place
called Guinea, beginning at
14 Degrees 30 Minutes

Lifted at random —
Clipped from the text of
A slaver's journal

where the English carry on
a River called Sherberow
Cape Lopez Gonsalves
River of Ancober to Acra
50 Leagues of Dutch Factories
consists in Negroes,
Elephants, Teeth, and other
Commodities

No, selected purposefully
Not randomly at all

smoke on the Sea-Shore
very barbarous and uncivilized
dissatisfactory account
durst venture himself
Old Callabar, where I
saw a sad Instance of
Child hung on the bough
taking off my Hat

fierce brutish Cannibals
Palm Wine and Milk in her Breasts

By me, my mind – from Snelgrave's journal
From Snelgrave's mind, a slave ship's captain

Freeport for all European Nations
thousand Negroes yearly exported
proud, effeminate, and luxurious
cut off his Head
large Sum of Money
Gentleman named Bullfinch Lambe
to make a Fetiche
imploring the Snake's Assistance
broiled them on coals

snippets of language, brutal and alive

Jeremiah Tinker, Esq.
Tribute in Loaves of Salt
dined under Cocoe-trees

infinite number of Flies

infinite number of Flies
dead Men's Heads
neck strings of Teeth
twenty shillings Sterling
in Cowrie Shells for every Man
struck him on the Nape
maimed Captives

Of all his words
these start to speak through me –
I hear them vibrating
they punch into my mind
and leave an ugly, pretty music

art of dying Goat Skins
divers Colours, for which
they make into Cartouche-boxes
Storehouses plundered
on himself by his Perfidy
Banditti of other nations

46

with sharp knives opened his
in several places and filled wounds
with a mixture of Limejuice,
Salt and Pepper

> *shingles of language, fragments*
> *left like broken shards*
> *of glass trinkets on the beach*
> *that still sing their bloody songs*
> *a history we know*
> *but now we hear it again*
> *in Snelgrave's 1734 voice,*
> *his severed words that still throb*
> *he is dead*
> *when you read these words*
> *you subvocalize*
> *your vocal cords vibrate*
> *even if you do not read aloud*
> *or utter a sound*
> *hear his words in your own voice*
> *these three hundred year old wordwounds*
> *whisper*
> *in your head my head*

Daughters to the King of Dahome
mud-walls, one Story high
Palm-Oyl took fire
antick dancing

> *antick dancing*

Hatchet in his Hand
small Cask of Beef
killed great Multitudes
to the Sugar Islands

> *Words that give*
> *"history" an iron taste*
> *of salted beef*

couple the sturdy Men
with Irons
forward on the Boom
happened at Barbadoes
twenty have hang'd themselves

twenty have hang'd themselves

Slaves from Mutinying
Blood requir'd Blood

Blood requir'd Blood

the Negro rashly struck
an Hour-Glass, just then turned
Rope fastened under his
shot to Death
Barricado on the Quarter-Deck
Muskets or Half-Pikes
Guns laden with Partridge Shot
eighty Negroes kill'd and drown'd

shaking brutal hurricanes
and mutinies at you
barbarous executions of Africans
rebellions and palm wine honey women
undersea live-burials
putrid neck ropes
scent of gunpowder
antic words biting like limejuice,
salt and pepper rubbed
into your blood-word-wounds

detained at Jamaica
Hurricane
contrary winds at Helvoet-Sluys
height of the Tide
Passage to the River Sieraleon
Latitude of 8 De. 30 Min.
they were morooned by him
Le Bouse, a Frenchman
black Flag at the Main-top-mast-head

three Leagues of the River's Mouth
roasting Oysters
fired pieces into the steerage
threw Granado-shells, which burst
his Chin almost cut off
Rogue, to slice my Liver
being dead drunk
Brent's Island, being the
Settlement of the Royal African Company

A drunken fly
Drink to drunkenness these words
that mapped slavery

WHEN MILES DAVIS PLAYS *PORGY AND BESS*

Stretched on my daybed
    with a rootbeer.
    Fifth grade.
Doxology for dusk, bass thrum.
I rest my face on the windowsill
to watch horses pastured
at the ranch across the way. Their cocked heels
point to Jupiter, low and bright,
leading the way. I think about
everything moody and forlorn
while Miles slides into the wow-wow
half-tones.

    I dream up details
    from some Saturday show: dogs, a river,
    torches, white Southerners' voices, fields
    burning black, wind burning water white;
    Bess   left behind,
    somebody's baby on her back.
    I don't know the musical tale
    or the DuBose Heyward book – just received
    images from Hollywood, the runagate.

    It will be years before
I learn enough about America
to pass up Gershwin's brooding French horns,
the simple folk plots of Heyward's sketch.
Years before a woman friend complains,
How can you listen to Miles?
He boxed his women around.

    I begin to play trumpet listening to Miles,
    trying to match his glides and bent notes,
    the emotional, drawn-out voice of his horn.

A girl trumpet player pinched, tripped,
kissed, beaten, and blasted in the ears
by the brass-playing boys in the band,

a fifth grade girl, dreaming
on summer nights to Miles' "Summertime".
From across a field, Porgy,
tarnished trumpet, dusty fedora
hanging heavy in his hands, calls out to me,
Bess, you is my woman now.
I want to open my screen door –
walk barefoot through lilac
blooms, and throw my arm
around his waist.

I love practising my trumpet
on summer nights, when the heady
smells of gardenias and mown grass
mixes with valve oil, spit,
and my own attempts at *Summertime,*
when the living is easy...

I like Miles' album photo,
the tight callused circle
distending on his lips from
intense years of pressure
against the mouthpiece.
I play until the bloody
rim of my lips tastes metallic.
By fall, two white scars raise
on my upper lip – railway tracks
leading away from a life
where living was easy.

THE BBC DOES BOMBA

Just a simple Saturday morning class,
Modesto Cepeda's hands on tanned-skin
barrel-drum, and his voice rising
in call and response with our smallest
niños trigueños, *Fuego,*
Fuego in Bucaná, Maximina
la Loca, Loca, ayyy!
Escuela de bomba
in the barrio, a one-room cement
cellblock where fat tías
deep-fry empanadillas in the back
and parents greet each other
with besitos in the carport.
Mothers bounce babies
on the breast to the clave beat
of the drum, clap, and sing.

Boys salute the drum,
toe the ground in fast cross-stepping,
fold arms in front of chest,
hold a beat,
then tremble
upright bodies
muscle by muscle
and sweep away from the drum,
bowing out
until a crooked-elbow
shoots arm up to a freeze-frame stop.

Girls raise the ruffled circle-skirt
to salute the drum, flick wrists
con fuerza until the butterfly skirts snap
por la derecha, por la izquerda,
the flower-print cotton

faldas swinging like machetes
over the harvest.

In the carnaval,
the children crawl around the drum,
cimarrones
plaiting their way through bush
and cane, "¡¡¡BOMBA!!!

But this week, the BBC brings
their camera crew and tripwires
and box-lights and monitors and
sound-boards and ex-Miss Mundo Puerto Rico
with her photogenic tetas in full-show
and an ancient wax-figure British gent
tortured by sweat and a sun never-hotter
yet this year. Those glum children
of the barrio (no matter how
the drums throb, and their
maestro sings his soul-raising
contralto to the ceiling)
tuck their hands into pockets
and folds of limp skirts,
courageously hiding their smiles from BBC.

The camera man curses,
I need it bigger, it isn't big enough.
The British gent tries to teach our best
boy-dancer some moves. He will
never see how that boy can quiver
just one back muscle,
holding others in glacial stillness,
until the worried drums break into a sweat.
A circle of adults shout, *¡¡¡Baila, baila, baila.!!!*
But the boy hooks his gaze on the window,
bites his tongue, and tugs on pants zipper

like it's a bell-rope – his dance, that!
The plantain-packed produce truck coughs
past before cameras can catch it.

Not big enough, not scenic and mangrove enough –
BBC packs up. British gent opens an umbrella
for his stroll of the musical neighbourhood.
At least they might crash up against some
thin neighbourhood men pushing rusting shopping
carts of detritus and dust, undernourished dogs,
banana trash, broken glass, and gutted furniture.
The producer coaches the gent's companion
for the neighbourhood amble, a bomba dancer.
Just talk about some of the greats that came from here,
you know, like Tito Puente or Tito Rodríquez,
or, I don't know, and how they were big
in New York during the Mambo years, and that
they came from here, but don't say too much.
The bomba man sighs, *I think Tito Puente*
came from New York.

Well, just talk
about some of the famous ones that came
from around here. Villa Palmeras?
The barrio? Puerto Rico? El caribe?
Or any place west of London, south of New York?

Last Saturday we put the baby-bouncer
of Modesto's three-month grandson
in front of his drum, and the girls brushed
their skirts over him. He kicked hard
for an hour and smiled. Might as well admit
that the palomas flew in from their ground walks,
and the sea eggs rolled in from Piñones,
and blue land crabs scuted out of the manglar,
and turtle grass flung itself outta the sea,
and black birds dropped their tostones

and came running, and the walls shined
like sugar crystals and grease, and the children
raised their hands, got on their knees, and danced,
laughing with Modesto's grandbaby, "¡¡¡BOMBA!!!"
Let the crisp British gent bellow and wheeze next to his Latin Miss Mundo
as they pick through rags on our streets.
They won't hear how the drums played
for the children *last* Saturday morning.
Let's hear it for the BBC *Historia de Bomba!*
¡BOMBA!

THE TWELVE-FOOT NEON WOMAN ON TOP
OF MARÍA'S EXOTIK PLEASURE PALACE
SPEAKS OF PAPAYAS, HURRICANES, AND WAKES

Look, with that scaffold up my back,
I was feeling Christ-like, like the stone Xavior
on the rock pinnacles of Río de Janeiro.
Felt like conducting the bloody symphony
of carnaval in Río's Sambodrome, or stalking
through the streets like Oya, orisha of whirlwinds
and cemeteries. Felt like flying to Guadeloupe,
Point-á-Pitre, where Kweyol rap booms through
the graveyards. Felt like landing on the black and white
checkerboard crypts of Morne-á-l'Eau.
Felt like it would free me from mourning you.
Felt like tasting of salt, and reggae, and rude boys.
Felt like sunning myself on the walls of the Fortaleza.
Felt like stretching my electric legs.
Felt like having daughters, big round brown
ones, who dance bomba in green skirts
and splash away from the crystalline jellyfish
and darting diamond angels of Aguadilla and Luquillo.
Felt like never cooking again, especially for you.
Felt like eating salty alcapurias con yucca y guineo.
Felt like banishing the tired crone in me, the one
begging Obatala for healing, patience, and wisdom.
Felt like riding a Shango train song all the way home,
letting the blues of it, and the R&B of it, and the funk
of it, and the beguine of it, and the mento of it,
and the quadrille of it rattle my hip bones to heaven.
Felt like starting a fire. Felt like starting a really big
conflagration to burn the urban plantation.
Felt like dressing in jumbie beads and silver.
Felt like tracking hurricanes, felt like drinking
tea of anise and lime peels. Felt like taking a bush bath
to cure the you in me. Felt like playing the cuatro

at a wake. Felt the Chupacabra in me rising –
Puerto Rican, blood-sucking soucriant.
Check it out. Nine thousand websites
have reported sightings of me, a creature
who terrifies Paso Finos in the fields, drains
the blood of fowls, ram goats, and pigs without
tearing flesh. The spines ridging my back
are raised. See the warning?
So I got down from the scaffold, baby,
and I switched off my neon tits, blink, blink...
When you call, I'm not home. I'm listening
to Stevie Wonder. I'm listening to my daughter
listen to Sister Carol who chats, singjay stylee,
about the natural jacuzzi I have in my rainforest backyard.
The flamboyán flames, the papayas are lush,
and neighbours give me star fruit and poma rosa by the bag.
Why did I let you bring me down, Papí?
Mamma and daddy only taught me how to sing
the blues; you taught me how to write them.
My only tears are for history, now.
Felt like wearing a cornflower blue dress, hem
trailing the water I walk on, tossing stars
into sea foam. Felt like weaving
Pennyroyale into my hair. Felt like writing
my son and daughter all my love songs –
each one ending with the words *Fyah burn*.

LADIES ROOM, CHICAGO BUS TERMINAL

Their make-up smeared, they've come here to sponge off,
to rake their children's hair, to slap them well,
collectively, that slap across the face
or on bare buttocks – they've been dying to
all the way down the highway, where the moon
stormed the bus window, and released prisoners
dozed, and the drunk woman in the front seat
bleated the gospel and sang. The length of
the highway, these women have been dying
to let it all out. They have felt the growl
rising like acid vomit in dry throats –
the fleshy desire to hit and hit
and hit until the hand is satisfied
and curls, a church glove in a coat pocket.
Women dragging their lives in taped suitcases
from one bus terminal to another
tow their children across the finish-line
of this room. Children tugged like goats on ropes
to the grimy sink, the spanking station
for these undomesticated ladies.
This is where they let it all out, where faults
of the tired child on the bus are tallied.
A kind of sanctuary where women
can snap, hiss, get right into the faces
of their children and howl venomous words.
Voices erupt on children trapped in stalls.
A kind of collective fury brought forth,
a complicity confined to this room,
where mothers don't wait to discharge their slaps.
Moms yell and yank their children up and down
in plain view while, one by one, women push
hand dryers on, then leave like guilty guards
who join looters but vow their innocence.
Whatever their final destinations

after Chicago, it's not the one they've
hoped for, before hope got in its Chevy
and barrelled out of their lives, vanishing
down the back roads of Iowa, past farms
and truckers' showers. One girl, post-whipping,
sits on a pillow astride her suitcase.
Hair uncombed, she looks like I did at five
when my mother, for crazed conduct, was strapped
into a bed at the state hospital.
Under fluorescent lights, she holds the wings
of an illustrated book. She shakes out
one hand that still feels a bone-bruising grip.
She wears shabby pajamas. I want to
read to her, gather her and my daughter,
both together, into my arms, or give
the smallest gesture that won't frighten her.
But her mother is in the stall, and what
would she say if she emerged and found daughter
clean and smiling? What if the girl was calm
and cradled one sweet dulce de coco from my satchel
in the safe haven of her uncrushed fingers?
I wash the thought away, dry hands, and flee.

PECKHAM, LONDON, COLD WATER FLAT

The last bus brings our men home from the night kitchens
while we feed her baby rice and Tabasco;
tie baby on the back with an African wrap,
and she sleeps. We watch British comedies
about bothersome, faded women, on the tele.
We break French and English trying
make sense of our lives, create our private pidgin.
On Saturdays we count coins, stroll Brixton market
to pick out yam, pepper, tomato, and a scrap of fish.
I buy pirate recordings of Stone Love Sound Clash.
When I'm leaving for good, going back to the Caribbean,
she brings me to her bedroom, where she unpacks *pagnes*
from home, Dutch Waxes, printed with flying fish
and stingray, and one green dress, fabric sheeny
with moon and star pattern when sun and shadow catches it.
Handpainted yellow cogs of colour wheel around the skirt;
uneven yellow rickrack adorns the neck.
A dress stitched in her Cote D'Ivoire. I will wear it
until the green fades to grey and patches of my skin
shine through thinning cloth. She brings out a pair
of embroidered satin high heels from Paris, impossibly
large for her feet or mine. She shows me how
she places paper in the toe to keep them in place.
I slide my feet in and try to raise myself
to that elevation. Feel the pinch of the paper.
Did she wear these shoes? They are beautiful.
The wadded paper, the way she helps me
hobble across the room to the mirror make them beautiful.
I will never wear them, but I place them in my bag,
promise to send American jeans and the hottest salsa music.
During the days, I have visited Notting Hill Carnival camps,
learned to play pan and sew parrot feathers, reasoned
with calypsonian Lord Cloak, drunk Carib with the sound-

lorry men and the women sewing spangles on spandex,
and interviewed a borough councillor who complained that
those West Indian riot-muckers pissed in his yard
and got too political with Carnival floats about Apartheid,
which went "like a swarm of bees" down the road.
At night, we have waited up together, both shy –
I, a guest in her home, a tramp picked up by her boarder
at an Africa Centre dance – grateful for a cold water flat
and kind lover to keep me warm. Her husband and my man, chefs,
work graveyard shifts and then ride the long night bus to Peckham.
Later, long after my good man goes off with an Italian gal
and I also travel to new, sadder romantic destinations,
the female friendship, of course, remains.
We exchange yearly photos of our daughters now and cards.
The yellow cogs on my worn-out green dress resemble
steel pan heads – I wear the music of London.
And I think of her and her warm cold water home.

GOOGLING THE CARIBBEAN SUBURBS

Sailor of the Sea of the Blue Screen,
dark terrace, ship's bow.
Night waves of the neighbourhood,
reverb of silence, insects' ensemble.
Shepherds and satos hushed.
No yellow flit of reinitas in bougainvillea.
Frog song thinning out to one coquí.
No human stuff stacked up.
No men on roofs, no men on lawns,
No men under the hiked-up hoods of cars,
No lawns to edge, no mouldy paint
to blast all Saturday with water jets.

Google space and the blue pearl appears;
plummet toward the cockroach droppings,
zoom to rainforest island, moving crabwise,
bomb's eye view of la ciudad de San Juan,
drive mouse through flat-top roofs
count concrete boxes on my block.
What global master-plan documents
my roof from space, my little Caribbean roof?

She struggles on the stairs, white flop-haired
elder, barefoot, rocking in thin housecoat
on a terrace next to mine, before dengue hours.
All morning she hacked with machete at the flowerbeds.
I saw her there as I rolled enamel glaze on leaves
to print a forest on my walls.
I have a mogote outside my bedroom window,
and the bush and banana encroach
on the gated streets where I live.
Homeless men live in the woods, and two starving horses,
and a family of pigs. When I see any of them there,

emerging from the tangled lane, I stop my car
to talk to them and look for rebellion in their eyes.

The Himalayas are melting.
Our flat-top roofs make a mirror grid.
A Sierra Club leader from the North
tells us we must add sloped roofs
to the slabs we live under.
The sea is rising in my neighbourhood.
We are nearly under water.
We are sitting on the roof.
Google Earth makes us out as small, blurred squares.
That's how we look, from out there.

WITNESS

Blue marlin jetting out of the sea,
a car heaves and jumps over the meridian,
convulsively coasting, a skiff beached
at the world's end of this gas station.
Motorcycle cop in pursuit
dismounts with baton in hand
like a white-hot father
ready to box a child down.
If he could harpoon the driver
and haul him out through the window,
he would. He beats the car door.
He wants the cabrón out of his car
right fuckin now.

An SUV swerves near the cop,
a woman shouting *Policia, abusador*!
but the cop hears only the sea-roar in his head.
He drags the driver ashore,
and I see it is a fisherman,
still in his rubber boots,
a hanging, wet t-shirt flecked with fish scales.
His car, not set in "park",
rolls downhill on its own, against traffic.
When the cop runs to catch it,
the fisherman walks randomly away,
as if on the surface of a light sea,
as if he has forgotten how to walk
on land that does not move under him.

When the policeman runs back to take the man down,
he clubs the fisherman hard in the kidneys on both sides.
With fast chop-strokes, he beats at the shoulders.
My daughter, standing by my side, asks *Do you see that?*
I nod. We see it.

No one at the gas station moves.
Men and women stand, serious and silent,
our lives fallen away from us.
No one tops off his tank and heads off.
We stay like watchmen.

The fisherman, on his feet still, flails as he is beaten.
Rock steady, mate.
I want to say that he strains
and leaps against the line
like a dorado, a dolphin fish,
golden and purple, leaping
from the sea, plunging and cutting
until he is tired, gaffed, and brought to the stern,
clubbed on the head until he quivers and is still.
But he is not a metaphor. He is just a fisherman
brought to the ground now
by another man, an off-duty cop in plain clothes,
who happens to be gassing-up his car here,
and who, without anger, and without addressing
the motorcycle cop, follows prescribed routine,
putting the *pescador* face down on the asphalt
with a knee in the back. He sits, straddling our fish,
and spreads out his arms flat to the sides.
When the arms weakly flap,
Plainclothes puts them firmly
and patiently down again three times
until they learn to be quiet.
The man's bleeding, moving jaw
still bites against the hook.

Like the flaming horses of Athena's chariot,
the SUV returns, the woman warrior,
100% Boricua and reckless
and shouting at the badjohn cop,
demanding name and badge number.

When she drives off, the two cops
gut the man's pants pockets,
dropping derelict items on the pavement.
When the syringe is retrieved,
the fisherman is handcuffed
and left face down on the street
until a police car comes.

If I stay with this metaphor,
you will see mahi mahi
well-cooked in una salsa sabrosa,
con ajillo, mantequilla, alcaparra,
served with amarillos, yellow fried plantains,
in a seaside Cataño restaurant,
not the man who was beaten at my feet.

I saw in that moment my students,
for a year now tear-gassed, pepper-sprayed,
beaten, kicked, groped on the breasts,
dragged and carried high in the air
by arms and feet like lechón
on a barbecue spit, and arrested
by an army-size troop of la fuerza de choque.
Sometimes I was there, close by
in the protesting crowd, helicopter overhead.
Sometimes I added mine to the thousands of hits
as I watched shaky cell-phone videos uploaded to websites.

Home now, I search my memory
for the video of Miguel Cáceres Cruz,
kicked and shot in the back of the head,
downed in the streets in front of El Playerito
in el barrio Punta Santiago, Humacao,
by police four years ago, sin compasión,
for the simple crime of safely directing traffic
at a quinceañera celebration.

I will tell you
that the people of this unfortunate isle
are dazed by police brutality.
How many times will we upload atrocities to You Tube?
How many times, in this tierra de los poetas,
will we trace the arc of the baton swing
in our reggaetón songs
before we all climb into our armoured and fiery SUVs,
a sea of la gente flooding past roadblocks
at La Fortaleza, banging on the windows,
chanting *We want el Señor Gobernador*
out of his mansion fortress
   to face us
     right
      fuckin
       now.

MEDITATING ON POLICE MADNESS
WHEN MORNING COMES

warm tea
con canela
window
leafless
tulip tree
soundclash!
green parrots bathe
in heavy rain
six rows of clouds
between here and the sea
green mountain in mist
pitrre in the flamboyán
paloma crowing on high wire
on top spire of a palm
black chango
roble drops pale pink blossoms
all around
sun quiets the day down
may every policeman on the island
start his day like this
blessed

BOSQUE SAN PATRICIO

I have come to this trail alone
at night, to the urban forest,
where my guide is the night sound
of owls and frogs of all sizes.
The small lantern
on my forehead
attracts insects
that drown themselves
in my eyes or veil
my face. To escape,
I switch off the beam,
a woman walking in a forest
at the base of a mogote
on a dark island surrounded
by the immense black sea.

I want to see the Puerto Rican boa
lunge from a tree
to devour a bat. I hope to see
a female curled in a puddle of water,
exuding pheromones
into the deep, green-tasting air
to invisible mates.
But I don't. I'm simply outnumbered
by frogs, coqui infants that fit
on a finger tip, large common frogs
with their bellies full
of snails. I crush
entire assemblies of snails
under my shoes
with loud popping noises
on the black path.

Time and abandoned shells, corals,
and sand turned to porous stone,
tiers of karst rounding into mountains,
receding seas and seeds dropped in faeces
of long-tongued bats and bobo birds,
forests of the mogotes,
caracoles – the land snails
still wearing conical hats
and spiralled shells
of their sea-born brethren,
snails dense on the night paths
of the dark forest
consumed by the gallon
by common frogs
and white-mouthed frogs,
and stepped on under
my feet.

The Tainos receded inland,
and mogotes were levelled
when the Irish farmed these lands,
and then the subdivisions
of flat-top cement box homes
were arrayed like a señorita's fan
at the base of the one surviving mogote.
Homeowners planted poma rosa, flamboyán.
When the nearby hospital closed,
houses were abandoned like old sea shells
and then bulldozed.

When the forest came down from the mogote,
domesticated, exotic trees went wild.
Green tangle overtook refrigerators, stoves,
toilets, and fire hydrants.
Now lizards sleep on the leaves.
I'm the only human animal.

But I still can't uncage myself.
I creep along the path,
under the massive branches
and listening monkey-ear
seed-pods of the guanacaste.
Every natural sound magnifies.
I use a stick to roll away the snails,
and slowly find my way back
to my car, my mattress,
my comfort zone, day and night
walled-up in cement.

NOONTIDE SAILOR SONG AND A BURIAL AT SEA

Shining herds of stone-skipping flying fish
skirt the prow of our skiff and hurdle three waves.
Doctor of the pueblo, we are saying goodbye.
Rest in our ferry, for we are feeding gold
and crimson petals to rare manatees in your name,
passing around the wine bottle. Look – the wet face
of the old man with a Castilian moustache – how he cries.
See the swells and troughs of his heaving shoulders.

Doctor of the pueblo, who, in truth, received
payments of white pigeons, eggs, and deep-fried bread
from los pobres of the pueblo, look at us here
in this bright boat. The large man with scarred knees
and the woman with a hairless patch on her crown,
they stare into the clear saltwater where starfish –
brilliant red, cream, mottled, speckled starfish – hunt
and actually race along the bottom. We hear
the propellers and look at the water's lattices of light –
where no one climbs to heaven, but your ashes drift down.

Doctor of the pueblo, you loved the sea.
The great mountains show their shadowed faces.
The dense palms of the coast arch and entwine.
Near Cayo Santiago, the monkey sentinels lope
along exposed tree roots and red clay,
carry off coco flowers, or come down near the edge
to place one hand in ocean surf – white-faced monkeys.
It is a good day. The young man in sports jersey
sits still behind his shimmering glasses. Pelicanos sit still
on their one dull ovenstone.

                    Doctor of the pueblo, you exist
in the oraciones shared in this craft, in the taste of wood ash
blowing into our throats, in the flotilla of margarita blooms

in our wake. The captain blows the conch three times.
Still my daughter sleeps, rocked by the hot engine.
Doctor of the pueblo, sleep. It is a good day
for curling up under the green, flowered quilt of the sea.
The cancer can't steal your breaths again. Sleep now.
Drift off. Gulp the balmy breeze.

PRODUCE TRUCK SUTRA

Heavy rain on the sea
drumming inland
rain-thrum
the thorn of sleep
pricking me to a last sweep
of dreams
the humpbacked
produce truck
blares its singsong
through the streets:
Guineo, manzana,
platano verde, yautía

A bowl of mountain coffee

The produce truck
brings me a memory
20 years ago
green tea ice cream
at the O-Bon
street festival
for the ancestors
Mexican bakeries
and cantinas
Buddhist temple –
harmony of the gong
Tonga drummers
beating the large casks
barrel drums
that once guarded
the sea entrances of Japan
pass booming
invitations
through our skeletons
to the dead

Hanamatsuri
birth of Sakyamuni Buddha
we ladle
sweet tea
over a golden god
rain came
on the day
he was born

The monk
delivers
the Sweet Potato Sutra
roots and runners
we send out
looking for the sun
our sweet, golden centres

I have journeyed
from place to place
sending out runners
In the Caribbean
our ancestors lie
in the sea
all around us
or they may be seen
from airplane windows
dressed as clouds
in colonial garb
slave labourers' dresses
in quadrille battles
above St. Vincent
and Barbados

Do the dead
arrive to the O-Bon fete
or the nine-night wake?

Do the dead rise
from sleep
sluggards
dragged awake
by drums
gongs
the amplified plea
of a produce truck?

Do the dead recover
from the violence
they did to each other in life?

With hair spiking
and nightgown
riding high
to the panty-line
I will stop
the produce truck
to buy an avocado
a lime and sea salt
I will sit
by the window
empty my mind
while the surf hisses
Ka-Shu
and avocado hulls
wreck at my feet

NIGHT WASH

We bathe in a wash tub, galvanized, because the bañera
won't drain and the landlady won't care and the plumber
sits under his lamp with a paper napkin and a pair
of tangerines and the shadowy caracoles and cemís of Corretjer's
poems dancing round in his head. My daughter first,
before the mosquito hours, soaped outside in the sunlight
and rinsed with cool bucket water laced with lemon grass.
I bathe later, when the sea turtle shell on the balcony
over the train station has given off its last marble
prophecies of loneliness for the day, and the blind dog
has followed the man who walks with a limp into the greater
darkness of Santa Rita alleys, and the sound systems
of El Ladrillo Bar have pitied the trembling window glass
and packed themselves away into the belly of the conga
that always stands, unplayed, in the corner, near the end
of the bar where los borrachos laugh and later rest their heads
on the domino table. Darkness falls, too, finally, on
our asphalt yard and concrete walls and the lithe bats folding
themselves into thorns. I pin a cloth around the tub's perimeter
and then tug off jeans, smell the mangrove swamps, brackish
and sweaty and salty and musky. I try to reach the crevices
that sing, *You are not the passion fruit of young loving, you of*
the boarded-up thighs, posted with signs, beware, beware;
you are not the moonlit beauty bathing under the streetlamp,
the bronze-haired one for whom the neighbours stand in darkness
behind their louvres, behind their prison bars of shadow
and moonlight, quietly watching her splash midnight water
on the lifted calf. No, you are the pendulum woman who looks
up at the tar patches and scrolling paint of the building
that the landlady doesn't care about, and you bathe yourself
in water without lemon grass. You might like gardenias
crushed and sluiced along your skin. You might like gardenias,
if the water was quite cold. Later, I trundle our clothes to the yard.
A cucaracha the size of my daughter does his laundry,

though I surprise him momentarily with my own basket
at the dryer we share. The night clerk at his hotel laughed
at the crease of grease around his collar, and so he is here,
emptying his coloureds, whites, and leopard underwear into
my Kenmore, his mind on erotica and the supple glistening
of his own shell. My rooms are dark and the night is dark –
the coquís amorous, but quiet, clinking their wine goblets
with a hush inside their wet, leafy tunnels. When one frog sings
alone, it sounds like someone weeping, or hiccupping after
the kind of hot-eyed, bottomless weeping that I have not had
for a very long time. The royal palms talked all morning
without end about what's brewing at sea – their grey, eaten
edges shock out black and still in the darkness, too.
I watch out for the junkie, the one with hair like a fur helmet.
Daily, he curses my generosities or insults violently, equally,
following me down the street, on my heels, rapping at my window,
Missy, Missy, Missy, Missy. I watch for him and other vagrants
who might be born for darkness and the night air as much as I,
who might carry metal instruments – hand-sharpened, curved,
which could sculpt my body into a shape unsuitable for mothering.
The cockroach mixes his silks with my cottons.
I watch the street, but I take time to find one star,
the only one that ever shines over my nothing-ever-works-
especially-the-plumbing home. I find it, and I sight it up – let its
cold light melt on the back of my neck like a shard of ice.
I feel the air on my wet, t-shirted skin. My laundry pal
likes the busy life, the legs burning, the dash, the eyes bloodshot.
I like the peace of the night. I like peace. At some time
in a woman's life, she likes peace. She likes to cool out that word
in her mouth, in the dark night air after a fresh night bath,
while her cold wash laundry spins, and her iced-tea glass leaves
circles of water on the glass table, and the shells on the shelf
start to sing to one another, but quietly, the outgoing surf,
not the shore-bound crash.

NOVENA A LA REINA MARÍA LIONZA

Noche primera

In las montañas de Sorte,
in a garden where Dios tends his begonias,
yellow-white nosegays for la reina Maria Lionza
de Venezuela, she tires of holding a human hip-bone
above the stalled motorists of Yaracuy –
for fifty barren years, a petrified emblem.
She grows bored of riding a tapir until her pum-pum
rubs raw from the statue's stiff contours. She desires
warm breath from 7th heaven, so a living snake
enters the iron helix encircling her ankles.
His copper coils clench and tug until la reina
feels sensation again. She arches back, nipples
pointed at the stars, a deity of la naturaleza
craving the diamond pinpricks of space.
Damballa eases into her until she pants, jaguar
in heat, and her casing splits. Concrete
and steel torso shattered, Maria Lionza slips free.
Papers vow it's a celestial sign that President Chavez will fail.
But she just has to wheel away, above la autopista
deadlocked around her feet, an obsidian anaconda.
She has to seek out what is still grass-green
in the cemetery cities of her El Dorado
and our islands, on earth's cement crust.

Noche segunda

In Yabocoa,
the winds catch a woman bathing in the storm.
Imagine, she just wanted a body-slam bracer of wet wind.
She wanted to be deluged and rocked in air alive all around her –
like those men who lash themselves to palm trees.

She wanted Huracán to breathe life into a manikin.
Instead gales coil her zinc roof into a tight watch-spring
and slingshot her hammock and bikini-body into the sky.
In the periódico, we see her deflated, buckled corpse
elegantly sprawled in her neighbour's gutter.
We see rows of prostrate plantains that spread out
their green hands over the flood waters like
devastated supplicants praying in a mosque.
What that news story does to me – a rag-doll woman
catapulted from her hammock into god's lungs!
Maria Lionza, Storm Jeanne is not done with us yet.

Noche tercera

In Puerto Rico, after
we have dreaded the spiral galaxies of hurricanes
travelling towards us at light speed in web satellite shots,
after the evil eyes of the storms have seen all that they want
of our island, we measure the nights in candle-hours.
Todo Puerto Rico queda sin luz y 500 mil abonados sin agua.
Yes, we are used to it. Still, each psyche is flooded.
In these weeks we hear radio news from our sister islands.
The bay and marina of red-roofed Grenada!
A ten-year-old girl drowned in Jamaica.
Gonaives, Haiti – trees used up for fuel and coal-pots,
nothing much to anchor soil when floodwaters came.
Families stranded in trees with no food. Two children
on a porch, their faces covered with cloths. The man in a flowered
dress watched his children and neighbours swept away.
The student begged soldiers to remove eleven bodies
floating in his house, four brothers and a sister.
When we may leave our homes, neighbours laugh
about the babies made in the storm: what else was there to do
sin luz? Babies made, babies lost in the storms.

80

Noche cuarta inmaculada

The ciclón remains, rumbling in the belly of a great boa constrictor.
The boa spends his mornings bumping the attic boards of a casita.
He passes secret nights smudging moist trails on the bedsheets
of a thirty-two year old girl who cannot speak.

Night after night after night, the great snake presses
his shape into her bedcovers, curling around the hot feet
of a woman with a child's mind and no speech.

Let us say that this woman lives with her mother
in the shadows of the green mogotes, the flooded hills
that conceal whatever creatures that still survive
the asphalt, strip malls, and jump-up election caravans.

In other casitas belligerent boas, made nervous refugees
by floodwaters, are cornered in bathrooms, bagged up
and hauled off. But this one goes undiscovered for days.
Imagine it, the nightly encounter. She can't talk.

And if the dumb beauty rides a tapir in the dark room,
or raises her own hip bones to the sky, or bathes
in nosegays of sun-white flowers, or sits
in simple contemplation of the massive snake,
her mother remains insensate to these developments.

For days the daughter studies the snake. He doesn't abduct her.
He doesn't consume her, burst, and birth her out,
a yellow African, Indio, Spanish water goddess
wearing jade pendant and pearls. He does not have articulate
human speech. He is silent, or hisses, or climbs trees.

Our woman listens to Damballa, but she does not become
la reina María Lionza de Puerto Rico y Venezuela.
Her figurine will not be sold at Botánica Santa Bárbara.
A benevolent lwa cannot carry messages to his children
through speech, esta chica cannot transmit his message.

Noche quinta

City of enemy hands,
City unconcerned with piety and purity of heart,
City that forgets its collapsed bridges y los árboles caídos,
City that forgets children sucked into floodwaters,
City that uproots, designs, executes, emits,
City of daily lucha, nightly struggle,
I had the desire today to lie on my back
under a turpentine tree on the ant-filled grass.
I wanted to see the wet leaves moving and the light.
I wanted succulent heat on my forehead and breeze.
I wanted to go to el jardín botánico
and lie down near green water and turtles,
let the sun create red hibiscus flowers on my inner eyelids.
But I didn't. The city kept beating me with its chiselled fists.
Can't I just lie down in my business suit under a tree?
When the light comes down in this city,
it does not illuminate
anything but leaves.

Noche sexta

What María Lionza said:
Follow the road in the belly of a snake,
through marsh saw-grass and Job's tears,
fragrant swamp flat-sedge and caña brava,
down to the manglar. Fiddler crabs

trace musical staffs along the salt flats –
violinistas and glazed flats the colour of sandstone.
Taste salt-crystal leaves of the black mangroves.
Colonies of red mangroves dip the dense brushes
of their aerial roots into the sea.
When the bright, reflective surface of the laguna
photographs the mangroves and clouds perfectly,
it makes a mirror I do not want to stop gazing into.

Noche séptima

A mute girl and a disoriented snake
made me think of María Lionza; made
me search music stores for the song
by Ruben Blades and Willie Colón;
made me listen to it on the car CD player
until my daughter could sing it;
made me walk Río Piedras, from
botánica to botánica, looking fruitlessly
for a figurine of La Reina María Lionza;
made me sleeplessly surf the internet,
where I found that her statue in Venezuela
had fallen apart that same week.
I did not find you, diosa de la naturaleza,
but you are the running vine binding my ankle.
Help me to shed my dead skin.
One botánica owner found a sheaf of prayers,
una novena a La Reina María Lionza.
He could only talk about the tropical depressions
still forming off of Africa.

Noche octava

We open the earth
with a little red shovel.
Red clay and worms.
A clay crater in la tierra.
She holds the sapling
close to her belly,
its roots paper-bagged.
An emajaguilla tree,
Spanish Cork, its already
dense crown of leaves
deeply heart shaped,
verde oscuro brillante.
Yellow-purple flame
flowers will bell out later.
My daughter and I
learn how to midwife
a tree of green hearts.
Un hoyo dos veces mas
ancho y el mismo profundidad
del envase de las raices.
We stake it and tie it.
We give it water.
It looks good to us.
Its trunk is a straight spine.
We have taken the time.
We have platforms of red clay
on our shoes.
She says, *I love this tree.*

Noche novena

An egg shell of the serpent, la ciudad de San Juan.
I want to chip it and crack it.
I've been inside a long time.
I want to star-gaze on the boardwalk of Piñones.
Daughter, look at the great storm brewing
now and always on Jupiter. Swing the scope
wide to our hills, to the snake-furrows
and side-winding valleys
of Earth where the birds flit up
and become stars. Dark now.
No rainbow after these storms.
Let us move away from the city's thunder.
Don't ask me for mall-debris
that a month later swells landfills.
Ask me for this: our night breaths sketching
vectors between sea and Orion's red shoulder,
our bodies revived by surf boom.
We'll raise miniature goats –
you'll feel their lips
nuzzling grains in your palm.
I want to grow you in a green-heart place
above the flood plains,
where after our terrible storms,
only roosters cry,
and, if we are blessed,
the serene snake
visits our bedrooms.
So we will live,
in sanctuary and light.

NOTES & GLOSSARY

"Cereus of the Night Passages" (pp. 11-12)

El Cristo de Buen Viaje: The Christ of a Good Voyage

Los pobres: the poor

El cuatro: stringed instrument with five double strings; in the guitar
family

Las palomas: doves

Los borrachos: the drunks

San Martín de los pobres: San Martín de los *Porres* is the Saint of the
poor

El Callejón: the alley

El Corazón: The Heart; name of a bar

El Callejón de la Capilla: Chapel Alley, located in Old San Juan

El aguacate: avocado

La Perla: the "pearl," a community on a narrow strip of land at the
bottom of a cliff and by the sea in Old San Juan, Puerto Rico

El cabrón: bastard; common insult

"La Madonna Urbana" (pp. 13-16)

Los Dos Picos: The Two Peaks; local name given to the architecture
of *la Iglesia de Dios Pentecostal*, a church in Barrio Obrero,
Santurce, San Juan, Puerto Rico

La Isla Encantada: Enchanted Island; Puerto Rico is popularly known
in Spanish as "La Isla del Encanto," the Island of Enchant-
ment

El Barrio Obrero: "*obrero*" means "worker"; a working class
neighborhood of Santurce, in San Juan, Puerto Rico

Donde las gomas usadas no tienen garantía: where used tyres are not
guaranteed

La bachata: popular music that has its origin in the Dominican
Republic

La gallina: hen; *Los pollitos*: chicks

La cancha de un residencial: the basketball court of a governmental
housing project

El Colmado Plaza Borinquén: Supermarket

Los petroglifos geométricos: geometric petroglyphs

El sabor del café del campo: the flavour of coffee from the rural areas

Boricua: Puerto Rican; may come from the Taíno name for the island, "*Borinquén*"

La cabrona: bitch

La Gata: Cat, also a nickname used by reggaetón diva Ivy Queen

Campesinos de las clases empobrecidas: peasants from the impoverished classes

A las tres de la madrugada: at three o'clock in the morning

Los disparos al aire: shots fired into the air

La Madonna boricua: Puerto Rican madonna

Lei Lo Lai: these vocables are frequently heard in the *mapayé* form of "*décimas*" (songs composed in poetic form and sometimes improvised in competitions) in the Puerto Rican troubadour (*el trovador*) tradition; thought to be Arabic in origin, arriving to Puerto Rico from Islamic Spain (*Al Andalus*)

Las mujeres somos putas y puercas: We women are whores and filthy

Busca para la vía de la esperanza: Look for the path of hope

Tienes que ser una mujer con pantalones: you have to be a woman who wears the pants; a woman with balls

Trigueño: refers to skin colour of person with mixed racial heritage; brown; a commonly-used racial demaracation in Puerto Rico

El velorio: a wake for the recently departed

El baquiné: traditional celebration held in Puerto Rico when a newborn infant dies; involves singing, feasting and drinking, and aids the child's soul to go to heaven (or cross over spiritually to the ancestral world); thought by some to have Afro-creole influences from the French Creole-speaking islands

Mamita, se ve bién, que linda eres: *Mamita* (what women and girls are called), you look good, how cute you are!

Mira, tengo hambre: Look, I'm hungry

Descansa: rest

alma, espíritu y cuerpo: soul, spirit and body

Pa'lante, Pa'lante, como un elefante: Keep moving forward like an elephant; common saying in Puerto Rico

Las caras lindas, las caras lindas, las caras lindas de mi gente negra. Oyeme, pero que bonitas son, lindas son, chulas son, bonitas son, lindas que son, lindas como tú verás, así son. Author's translation: The lovely faces, the lovely faces, the lovely faces of my black people. Listen to me, but how beautiful they are, how lovely they are, how sweet they are, beautiful, lovely they are, lovely, as you will see, that's how they are.

"The First Day of Hurricane Season" (p. 17)

El flamboyán: tree of the species *Delonix regia,* known in English as the Royal Poinciana or Flamboyant tree; common and beloved tree in Puerto Rico

"El Velorio, The Wake (1893)" (pp. 18-20), a wall-sized canvas by Francisco Oller, depicts an infant's country wake, or *baquiné*, and is Puerto Rico's best known painting.

Los jíbaros: refers to the people who live in-land or in the hills and mountains of Puerto Rico; hard working agriculturists with an independent spirit, connected to the land and traditional living; valorized as a symbol of Puerto Rican identity; as it might be said in Jamaica... people who "*come from country*"

El baquiné: (see above)

Los Tainos: Pre-Columbian indigenous residents of Puerto Rico, thought to be related to the Arawaks; also thought to have originally migrated to the Caribbean region from Venezuela or other parts of South America

El güiro: rhythm instrument made from a hollow marimbo gourd scored with parallel grooves on one side and played by scraping a metal fork against the grooves

La bala perdida: stray shot; stray bullet

Me voy a morir: I am going to die

Miren a mi bebé, ella es mi hijita querida: Look at my baby, she is my darling little daughter

La abuela: grandmother

"Snort This" (pp. 21-23)

Los pájaros: birds

La guanábana: soursop

El arroz con gandules: rice and pigeon peas

El agua: water

La Comadre: godmother; co-mother; woman who befriends a family and helps the mother with the raising of her children or child-related tasks; social practice by women, which provides mutual support in the daily routine

"By the Waters of St. Lucia" begins with a quotation from St. Lucian poet and playwright Derek Walcott's poem "The Star-Apple Kingdom".

SIDA (sínodrome de inmunodeficiencia adquirida): HIV/ AIDS

El Nuevo Día: Puerto Rican daily newspaper

"Canute Caliste" (pp. 28-29) is set in Carriacou, the Grenadines, in the Windward Islands. The painting described, "My Memory Alwy There", may be seen in the book *The Mermaid Wakes: Paintings of a Caribbean Isle by Mr. Canute Caliste,* London and Basingstoke, MacMillan Education, Ltd., 1989. Maurice Bishop played a leading role in the New Jewel Movement, served as Prime Minister of Grenada and was assassinated during a battle between revolutionary factions at Fort Rupert. Shortly thereafter, the US military invaded Grenada.

The poem **"Matron"** refers to the People's National Party leader Michael Manley, a late Prime Minister of Jamaica. The term "Twelve Tribes" refers to a house of Rastafari.

"Going Up, Going Down" (pp. 32-36)

El besito: brief, light kiss; kiss given on the cheek in greeting

Saludos: greetings; said as a form of cordial address when two people meet

Batty bwoys: a pejorative term for homosexuals in Jamaica

Los patos: literally "ducks', a pejorative term for homosexuals in Puerto Rico

Papí: term of endearment used for men and boys

As the poem explains, **"Two Women Chatting by the Sea" (1856)**, (pp. 38-40) was painted by Camille Pissarro, the impressionist artist born on the Caribbean island of St. Thomas. José Julián Martí Pérez (1853-1895) was a Cuban essayist, poet, journalist, professor and revolutionary leader who fought to end colonialism in his homeland. Trinidadian-born C.L.R. James (Cyril Lionel Robert James) (1901-1989) was an important Marxism-influenced Caribbean theorist, historian and novelist. Frantz Fanon (1925-1961), an activist, psychiatrist, philosopher and revolutionary in Algeria, was born in Martinique. He wrote the influential texts *The Wretched of the Earth* and *Black Skin, White Masks.*

"Caribbean Art" (p. 41)

El tren urbano: elevated and underground subway train of Puerto Rico

El Yunque: Puerto Rico's tropical rain forest near the Luquillo; part of the Northeast Ecological Corridor

"Reading Krik? Krak! in Puerto Rico" (pp. 42-44)

La Torre: the clock and bell tower on the campus of the University of Puerto Rico; modeled on *La Giralda*, the bell tower of the *Catedral de Santa María* in Seville, Spain

Conjunto de Clarinetes: Clarinet ensemble

Los trovadores: troubadours, in this case of the "*Tuna*", a university musical group; Tunas exist in the universities of Spain, the Netherlands, Portugal, Central and South America, and Puerto Rico; the clothing of the Tuna, called *el grillo* (or the "cricket"), is derived from Iberian students of the 16th and 17th century and includes a cloak, a "*beca*" (a sash decorated with ribbons and spoons, a doublet, bloomers, and leg stockings

La mariposa negra: black butterfly

La Guardia Costera: the U.S. Coast Guard

La botánica: store selling ítems related to *espiritismo*

Los deambulantes: homeless people

El espiritismo: spiritual and material practice influenced by the French linguist, educator, mystic and philosopher Allan Kardec (Hippolyte Léon Denizard Rivail, 1804-1869)

La Borinqueña: national anthem of the Free Associated State of Puerto Rico; there are two versions of the lyrics, one written by Lola Rodríguez de Tió and one by Manuel Fernández Juncos; the version written by Rodríguez is associated with *el Movimiento independista puertorriqueño*

Nationalistas: those who associate with *El Partido Nacionalista de Puerto Rico* or those who seek to make Puerto Rico an independent republic

For the text referenced in **"Language and the Mapping of Slavery"** (pp. 45-49), see William Snelgrave. *A New Account of Some Parts of New Guinea. I. The history of the late conquest of the Kingdom of Whidaw by the King of Dahomé. II. The manner of how the negroes become slaves. III. A relation of the author's being taken by pirates.* Gale ECCO, Print Editions (June 16, 2010).

"Listening to Miles Davis Play *Porgy and Bess*" refers to the DuBose Heyward novel *Porgy* (1925) and the opera version, *Porgy and Bess,* scored by George Gershwin.

"The BBC Does Bomba" (pp. 52-55)

Los niños: children

Maximina la Loca, Loca es: traditional bomba lyrics; in the Fiesta de Santiago Apóstol (St. James), a street festival and procession held annually in the Puerto Rican *pueblo* of *Loíza,* the carnivalesque character of *"la loca"* is a man dressed as a "crazy" woman with an exaggerated padded bottom and breasts, who flirts with observers and sweeps the dust of the streets into a large cracker tin with a broom made from the branching spikes and inflorescence of the coconut palm tree

Fuego, Fuego in Bucaná: traditional bomba lyrics

La tía: aunt

Las empanadillas: in Puerto Rican Creole cuisine, a deep- fried pastry turnover filled with meat, crab, cheese, a pizza-flavoured mixture, etc., known in Jamaica as *patties*, in India as *samosas* and in Trinidad and Tobago as *aloo pies*

Clave: percussion instrument comprised of two short, thick wooden sticks, often made of hard rosewood that the player strikes together to establish the "clave beat"; syncopated musical rhythmic pattern originating in Sub-Saharan Africa and found in Afro-Cuban and Puerto Rican music, including the *rumba, son, mambo, salsa, Latin jazz, songo and timba*

Con fuerza: with force

por la derecha: to the right (the movement of a full-circle bomba skirt)

por la izquerda: to the left (the movement of a full-circle bomba skirt)

La falda: skirt

Los cimarrones: African Maroons

Las tetas: impolite term for women's breasts

Baila, baila, baila!!!: dance, dance, dance

Piñones: coastal area on the North side of Puerto Rico, located between Playa Carolina and Loíza, lined with food kiosks, some of which cook over open wood fires

El manglar: mangrove swamp

Los tostones: slice of green plantain fried, smashed into a flat circle and fried again until crisp; eaten with mayo-ketchup

"The Twelve Foot Neon Woman on Top of Marla's Exotik Pleasure Palace Speaks of Papayas, Hurricanes, and Wakes" (pp. 56-57) makes a reference to the legendary Puerto Rican vampire-like creature the Chupacabra, or goat-sucker. "Shango Train Song" is a phrase coined by Bajan poet Kamau Brathwaite (See Appendix VII of *Barabajan Poems*). The phrase "rattle my hip bones to heaven" alludes to Brathwaite's poem "Negus" In *The Arrivants*. "Fyah burn!" is a Rastafari phrase used to chant down the forces of injustice.

La Chupacabra: literally "goat-sucker"; a mysterious creature that purportedly punctures the neck of its prey with two fangs and drains the animal of blood without tearing the flesh; many livestock deaths have been attributed to the *chupacabra* in Puerto Rico

La Fortaleza: the first defensive fortress built in San Juan and the official residence of the Governor of Puerto Rico; built between 1533 and 1540 near the harbor of San Juan

Los Paso Finos: elegant Puerto Rican horse breed known for its proud-bearing and four-beat gait

La poma rosa: pear-shaped fruit with red skin and white flesh; known in the English-speaking islands of the Caribbean as Otaheite apple, Malay apple or pommerac

"Ladies Room, Chicago Bus Terminal" (pp. 58-59)

Dulce de coco: candy made with grated coconut, coarse cane sugar or brown sugar, and, sometimes, almonds

"Peckham, London, Cold Water Flat" (pp. 60-61)

Pagne: wide-loom printed African cloth. Dutch Wax fabrics are highly regarded for their quality of weave, printing and design.

"Googling the Caribbean Suburbs" (pp. 62-63)

El sato: stray dog

La reinita mariposera: refers to the *Dendroica adelaidae*, a yellow-bellied bird that is also known as the bananaquit or Adelaide's warbler

El coquí: *Eleutherodactylus coqui*; small, singing frog and symbol of Puerto Rico; the frog's onomatopoeic name imitates the sound that it makes: co-quí

"Witness" (pp. 64-67) borrows from Ernest Hemingway's descriptions of fishing in *The Old Man and the Sea* (1952)

El pescador: fisherman

con ajillo, mantequilla, alcaparra: a sauce with garlic, butter and capers

Los amarillos: soft and crispy plantains fried yellow-brown

Una salsa sabrosa: a delicious sauce

La fuerza de choque: riot police
El lechón: pig roasted whole on a barbecue spit
La tierra de los poetas: the land of poets
La quinceañera: celebration held when a girl reaches 15 years old
El Señor Gobernador: the Honorable Governor

"Noontide Sailor Song and Burial at Sea" (pp. 72-73)
Las oraciones: prayers
La margarita: *Chrysanthemum leucanthemum*, the flower also known as
a "daisy"

"Night Wash" (pp. 77-78) mentions the Puerto Rican poet Juan
Antonio Corretjer, author of *Yerba Bruja* and several other books.
The term "Cemi" refers to spiritual forces and figures carved by
Tainos, the Pre-Columbian indigenous people of Puerto Rico and
other Caribbean islands.
Cemis: carved anthropomorphic, zoomorphic or anthropo-
zoomorphic artifacts that are thought to embody or represent
Taíno gods, spirits or ancestors
La bañera: bathtub

"Meditating on Police Madness When Morning Comes" (p. 68)
La canela: cinnamon
El Chango: *Quiscalus niger brachypterus*, black bird also known as the
Mozambique or the Greater Antillean Grackle
El Pitrre: *Tyrannus dominicensis*, also known as the grey kingbird,
petchary and tyrant flycatcher
El roble: *Tabebuia rosea,* tree shrub with numerous bell-shaped
flowers, also known as the Poui or Trumpet Tree

"Bosque San Patricio" (pp. 69-71)
El árbol de Guanacaste: *Enterolobium cyclocarpum,* known as the
Monkey Ear Tree because of the shape of its seed pods
Bobo: refers to the bird *Coccyzus minor*, known as the *Pájaro bobo
menor* in Puerto Rico, also known as the lesser cuckoo or the
mangrove cuckoo
Los caracoles: snails

"Produce Truck Sutra" (pp. 74-76)

Guineo, manzana, platano verde, yautía: banana, apple, green plan-
   tain, malanga root

"Novena a La Reina Maria Lionza" (pp. 79-86)

La noche: night; *La novena:* a nine-part, or nine-night prayer; *La reina*:
   the queen

Noche Prima:

La naturaleza: nature
pum-pum: rude Jamaican word for the vagina
La autopista: freeway

Noche Secunda:

Huracán: god of the storm, also known as "Juracán" by the Taínos,
   Pre-Columbian indigenous inhabitants of Puerto Rico and
   some of the sister islands
El periódico: newspaper

Noche cuarta immaculata:

El ciclón: cyclone
La casita: traditional wooden-frame house of Puerto Rico
La chica: girl

Nocte Quinta:

Los árboles caídos: fallen trees
El jardín botánico: botanical garden
La lucha: the struggle; can signify a resistance movement or just the
   everyday struggle of life
Todo Puerto Rico queda sin luz y 500 mil abonados sin agua: all of
   Puerto Rico is left without electricity and 500 thousand are
   without water

Noche Sexta:

La caña brava: tall, vigorous and dense-growing wild cane grass of the
   species of *Gynerium sagittatum*; also known as "bitter cane"

Las violinistas: fiddler crabs

Noche Septima:
La diosa: goddess

Noche Octava:
La emajaguilla: *Thespesia populnea*, also called Spanish cork or Portia
       tree, in the mallow family, native to Africa and common in
       India, with glossy, heart-shaped leaves and hibiscus-like
       flowers; grows in coastal areas of the Caribbean; in some areas
       of the Pacific, the tree is considered sacred and is grown near
       temples; the leaves have a medicinal use for treatment of skin
       problems, wrinkles and lice
Verde oscuro brillante: dark, brilliant green
Un hoyo dos veces mas/ ancho y el mismo profundidad/ del envase de las raíces:
       A hole twice as wide as and the same depth as the container of
       the roots.

Noche Novena:
La ciudad: the city

ABOUT THE AUTHOR

Loretta Collins Klobah lives in San Juan, Puerto Rico, where she is a professor of Caribbean Literature and creative writing at the University of Puerto Rico. She has lived in various locations related to the Caribbean experience, including Jamaica, England, and Canada. She earned an M.F.A. in poetry writing from the Writers' Workshop at the University of Iowa, where she also completed a doctoral degree in English, with an emphasis on Caribbean literary and cultural studies. She was one of eight poets featured in the anthology *New Caribbean Poetry*, edited by Kei Miller (Carcanet Press, 2007), and her poetry has also been anthologized in the 1996 *Pushcart Prize Anthology, TriQuarterly New Writers*, and the collection *How Much Earth?* Her poetry and scholarly essays have been published widely in the Caribbean, the United Kingdom and the United States of America, with poems appearing in such journals as *The Caribbean Writer, Poui: The Cave Hill Literary Annual, TriQuarterly Review, Quarterly West, Black Warrior Review, The Missouri Review, The Antioch Review, Cimarron Review* and *Poet Lore*. In addition to the Pushcart Prize and various awards from literary journals, her poetry has received the Earl Lyons Award from The Academy of American Poets and the Pam Wallace Award for an Aspiring Woman Writer. She was also the recipient of a tuition scholarship at the Bread Loaf Writers' Conference at Middlebury College in Vermont.

NEW POETRY FROM PEEPAL TREE PRESS

Shara McCallum
The Face of Water: New and Selected Poems
ISBN: 9781845231866; pp.: 140; Pub., October 2011; £9.99

Since the publication of her first collection, *The Water Between Us*, Shara McCallum has steadily created a rich body of poems that have mined the rich deposit of emotional and intellectual capital found in her background of multiple migrations, culturally and geographically. McCallum's poems reflect her rooting in a Jamaican experience unique for her childhood in a Rastafarian home filled with reckless idealism, the potential for profound emotional pathology, and the grounding of old folk traditions. Her work has explored what it means to emerge from such a space and enter a new world of American landscapes and values. *The Face of Water* collects some of Shara Mccallum's best poems, poems that establish her as a poet of deft craft (and craftiness), whose sense of music is caught in her mastery of syntax and her ear for the graceful line. She manages in these poems to enact the grand alchemy of the best poems – the art of transforming the most painful and sometimes mundane details of life into works of terrible and satisfying beauty. McCallum demonstrates eloquently her debt to the poetics of the Caribbean and of North America, even as she establishes herself as a vital voice in the later tradition of poetry written in mutable language, English. As poet she feels no hesitation about turning that language into a very personal music. *The Face of Water* is an excellent introduction to the poetry of Shara McCallum, a vital and exciting poet of pure elegance.

Kwame Dawes
Wheels
ISBN: 9781845231422; pp. 205; Pub. October 2011; £9.99

In *Wheels*, Kwame Dawes brings the lyric poem face to face with the external world in the first part of this century – its politics, its natural disasters, its social upheavals and ideological complexity. If these poems are political it is because, for Dawes, politics has become a compelling part of human experience. The poems in *Wheels* do not pretend to have answers, nor are specific political questions seen as especially fascinating. Dawes's core interest remains the power of language to explore and discover patterns of meaning in the world around him. So that whether it is a poem about a near victim of the Lockerbie terrorist attack reflecting on the nature of grace, or a president considering the function of art, an Ethiopian emperor lamenting the death of a trusted servant in the middle of the twentieth century, a Rastafarian in Ethiopia defending his faith at the turn of the twenty-first century, a Haitian reflecting on the loss of everything familiar, these are poems seeking illumination, a way to understand the world.

Dawes frames the sequence around the imagined wheels of the prophet Ezekiel's vision, and then he allows himself the post-modernist liberty of pilfering images from Garcia Marquez's novels, accounts of slave rebellions, passages from the Book of Ezekiel, the current overwhelming bombardment of wall-to-wall news, and the art of modernist painters, to create a striking series of songs that are as much about the quest for love and faith as they are about finding pathways of meaning through the current decade of wars and political and economic uncertainty.

In the end, the poet as prophet knows he is never assured of full illumination or clarity, but the fascinating metaphor of wheels, interlocking and unlocking, provides us with moments of luminosity and sheer beauty.